D1073591

SUPER ROUTINES OF THE SUPER STARS

Hot Training Cycles for Ultimate Muscle Growth!

By Robert Kennedy and Dwayne Hines II

613.713
KEN

Copyright © 1997 by Robert Kennedy

All rights reserved, including the right to
reproduce this book or portions thereof
in any form whatsoever.

Published by MuscleMag International
6465 Airport Road
Mississauga, Ontario
Canada L4V 1E4

Designed by Jackie Kydyk
Edited by Brett Nelson

Canadian Cataloguing in Publication Data

Kennedy, Robert, 1938-
   Super routines of the super stars: hot training cycles
for ultimate muscle growth

Includes bibliographical references and index.
ISBN 1-55210-005-7

   1. Bodybuilding--Training. I. Hines, Dwayne, 1961-
II. Title.

GV546.5.K46 1997   646.7'5   C97-900481-0

10 9 8 7 6 5 4 3 2 1

Distributed in Canada by
Canbook Warehouse
Newmarket, ON
L3Y 7V1
800-399-6858

Distributed in the United States by
BookWorld Services
1933 Whitfield Park Loop
Sarasota, FL 34243
800-444-2524

Printed in Canada

This book is not intended as medical advice,
nor is it offered for use in the diagnosis of any
health condition or as a substitute for medical
treatment and/or counsel. Its purpose is to
explore advanced topics on sports nutrition
and exercise. All data are for information only.
Use of any of the programs within this book is
at the sole risk and choice of the reader.

Bruce Patterson

SUPER ROUTINES OF THE SUPER STARS - Hot Training Cycles for Ultimate Muscle Growth!

Table of Contents

Chapter Four

Chapter Five

Alq Gurley

CHAPTER ONE

Why Cycle?

then it ceases to move ahead and instead moves into a maintenance mode. The body is moving to balance its full work capacity, and growing muscle is not necessarily its number-one function. So it grudgingly gives some support to the muscle-building function, but quickly ceases. This reluctance of the body to build muscle mass beyond a basic level means that you have to work hard at provoking the body to produce. The body becomes familiar with the routine and moves from a muscle-building mode into a maintenance mode. Familiarity breeds contempt from the physique.

Moving Out of the Maintenance Mode

If you want to make new muscular gains, you have to move out of the maintenance mode and into the growth mode. This is not an easy thing to accomplish. One way to do this is to add more weight to the barbell, dumbell, or weight machine. This new challenge stimulates the body to new growth. But simply adding weight to the bar is not always the perfect answer. You have to deal with a variety of factors and adding weight to the bar is only one of several effective techniques for pushing the body to a new spurt of growth.

Why cycle? Better yet, what is a cycle, since not everyone who works out is familiar with the cycling concept. A cycle is a certain type of workout routine performed over a certain period of time. The period that a cycle is performed for may last from a few weeks to several months – sometimes even longer than half a year. A cycle is a training routine set up to achieve a certain result.

One of the primary reasons a cycle is used is to stimulate the body into new muscular growth. The human body seeks to move to a level of efficiency. It will only build muscularity to a certain point for each level of stimulation,

Kevin Levrone, Dorian Yates and Nasser El Sonbaty

Lee Priest

Using a cycle is how you make the most of your physical potential. A cycle is a specific group of exercises used to achieve a specific result. The arrangement of the exercises and other supporting items also play a part in setting up the training cycle. Cycling is an excellent way to control your training and your physique, which should be your aim.

A training cycle keeps the body moving ahead in a guided manner.

Variety

If you notice, the introduction on cycling is somewhat vague. And it is designed to be that way. The reason is that with a training cycle, you have a tremendous amount of latitude. You are not stuck with just one item on your plate – you have a vast menu to choose from. As mentioned earlier, a training cycle is a specific group of exercises put together to achieve a specific result. That is a good static definition of a training cycle, but what makes up those specific exercises is not so static. You can incorporate any of dozens and even hundreds of exercises into your cycle. And you can use other factors such as the repetition range, the number of exercises, the number of sets, the speed of the motion, and the angle of the motion, to change any training cycle. Your options are vast. So a training cycle is "a specific group of exercises put together to achieve a specific result," but you decide what the specific result is that you want, and then the group of specific exercises that will achieve that result. Just how do you do that? This book will provide you with enough options for you to choose the workout cycle that you

Cycling

Perhaps the best tool of all for continually keeping the body on the cutting edge (and therefore growing in muscularity) is the cycle. A training cycle keeps the body moving ahead in a guided manner. A cycle is a detailed method of producing muscle growth. Of course, you can get some growth with a nonspecific or hit-and-miss approach to training, but the gains you do get will soon cease. And any gains that you attain through a haphazard approach to training will be minuscule compared to what you could have done had you used a specific cycle instead.

want. The following chapters have some of the best cycles known.

Correct Order

There is a correct order in which to go about preparing and then using a training cycle. The order is to first choose the specific result that you want from your training cycle, then choose the specific exercises (and exercise arrangement) that will give you those results. Often people get this mixed up and choose certain exercises without really giving any deep thought to why they are using them. That is like putting the cart in front of the horse, or pulling the trigger of a gun before you have a target to shoot at. You must know what you want to achieve with your training to get the most out of your cycle and to come as close as possible to maximizing your full physical potential.

Kevin Levrone, Vince Taylor and Paul Dillett battle it out!

The correct order in which to use the training cycle:

1. Aim at specific results that you want to achieve.
2. Choose the exercises that will produce those results.
3. Mix in the right arrangement of the exercises, including the right amount of sets, repetitions, etc.
4. Don't forget the supporting factors such as rest and recuperation when setting up a cycle.

Once you know what you want to do with your physique, and how you want to shape your muscularity, you can then go about finding the best training cycle to do just that. Perhaps you want to build a bigger chest. You can custom tailor a training program to achieve that result. The same is true with the other bodyparts. You can take aim at your arms, upper and/or lower legs, upper torso, or waist and literally change the way they look through a good training cycle.

Jay Cutler

Written Goals

A goal is a powerful tool for achieving anything in life. This applies to the world of the physique as well as the business world and other areas. Goals can help you move mountains. One author writes:

"Goals and plans are magic keys to success. Only three percent of all people have goals and plans and write them down. Ten percent more have goals and plans, but keep them in their heads. The rest – 87 percent – drift through life without definite goals or plans. They do not know where they are going and others dictate to them. Let's examine these statistics further. The three percent who have goals and plans that are written down accomplish from fifty to one hundred times more during their life than the 10 percent who have goals and plans merely kept in their heads. These statistics alone should motivate you to set definite personal goals, establish a plan of action, and then commit both your goals and plans to writing."[1]

These dynamic thoughts apply to the way you train your body as well as in other areas of life. You need a written goal and plan. A training cycle is all about setting a goal and a plan on how to get there (through exercise). You can successfully start your cycle program by committing it to paper – putting your goals and plans down in solid form.

> Some of the most effective tools for positive change are goals and plans, especially if they are written down.

Some have noted that "the thinnest line is better than the thickest memory." A written goal gives you unfailing direction, even when you forget your initial aim. And a written goal is both a commitment and a challenge – a commitment to reaching the goal, and a challenge to stick to the plan and endure until you achieve your goal.

A written goal is both a challenge and a commitment.

The Best

Once you have determined what specific results you want, and have set a goal to aim at, if you are wise, you will take the best path to that goal. Why mess around with second best? Time is a precious commodity and you don't want to waste it on ineffective routines. An ineffective training routine is not much more than wasted time. What you want is the routine that will do the job, and do the best job possible. This is especially true when it comes to building muscle. The body will not respond significantly unless it is pushed into a certain "zone" where the muscle gains come from. And you will have a hard time getting into this training zone unless you employ a first-class training cycle.

Hot Cycles

Where do you find these "hot" cycles? You find them from the people who use cycles all of the time and know what works and what doesn't work. These people are professional body-builders. A professional bodybuilder depends upon his training cycle to work to achieve the goal he wants. A professional bodybuilder lays a year or more of training effort on his training cycle, using it to prepare his body for the ultimate competition(s). When you spend a year or so preparing for a contest, you place a lot of weight upon your training cycle. And often big money rides on the effort, too. So the professionals really know their cycles – they have to.

Not every professional bodybuilder auto-matically knows how to put together a training cycle (sometimes a coach, trainer, or physique writer may have a better grasp of the situation) but the professionals know how to get what they need and then use it. Sometimes it is observation, sometimes it is from reading, and sometimes from word of mouth, but the pros get what they need. And over time they compile a mental data bank that they can draw upon for the firepower they need at just the right time.

Dorian Yates

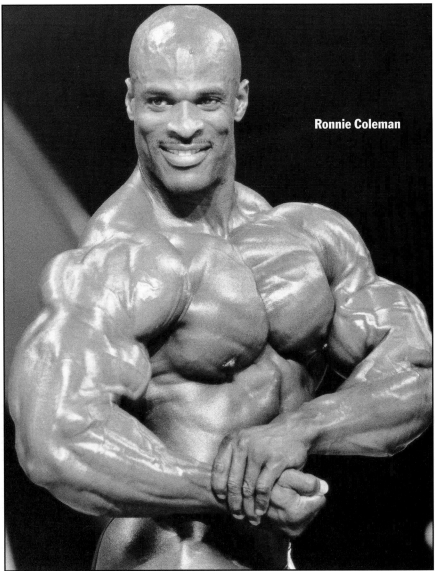

Ronnie Coleman

Routines of the Super Stars, which is a compilation of many of the routines of the top stars. This book puts a variety of the champion's training routines at your fingertips.

The Right Routine

It is important to find the right routine for your needs. As you use this book keep that in mind. Some of the super routines of the super stars are for putting on muscle bulk, some are for contest preparation, some are specialty routines for dealing with a bodypart that needs to be brought up to par. Pick the super cycles that will help you achieve the goals you want.

You may not have a totally clear goal of what you want. Not everyone does. You can use the different training cycles to find out what works best for your body. Use the different routines to explore the muscular responses of your body. However, it is best if you can aim at a specific target. Once you have the target to aim at, align yourself with a training cycle that can help you attain your goal. Select a cycle that focuses on the same target that you want to hit.

Not For Beginners

Although there will be a few routines for someone just starting to work out, most of the super routines of the super stars are more advanced in nature. Keep that in mind when you are picking out the cycle that you are going to use.

Some of the routines are centered around the champion's preparation for a contest. This can be particularly helpful and provide insight for you if you are planning on participating in a contest. However, that is not the only function these types of routines provide. You can use a champion's contest routines to become lean and mean and look good for summer, or to trim down on fat and build up your muscularity because that is the main goal of contest preparation. You do not have to use every exact detail. You can get the main points of the champion's workout and put it to use for yourself.

The off-season is another definite training approach for the champion bodybuilders. During this time many add more muscle mass and overall size. Others specialize on certain bodyparts, blasting certain muscle groups

No Exclusivity

You can use these hot routines also. There is no law that says they belong exclusively to the professionals. You will not be arrested if you use them in your routine. So feel free to use any training routine that you want.

You can use any routine that you want to.

Where do you find these hot routines? Often you will find them in a bodybuilding magazine. Or you can observe them in the gym if you happen to be fortunate enough to workout where a champion does. Another option is to buy the training videos of the champions. But that can be expensive, especially at around $30 to $40 or more per video. Best of all, you can use this book, *Super*

while taking it easy on others. These types of cycles will also be included in this book.

Whatever your aim, you can probably find a cycle in this book that will help you get to where you want to go. And you don't have to use one cycle exclusively – you can mix a couple, or take a few exercises from two or three cycles and put them in one new cycle of your own making.

Physique Philosophy

When it comes to training the body, not all of the champion bodybuilders have the same philosophy. You may notice some very different approaches to training among the different champions. Some bodybuilders use a type of training that is the opposite of another champion, but both of their physiques are awesome. Different training works differently for each individual. Some bodybuilders find a workout cycle that puts them in a certain "groove" and they stay with that style for a long time. Others experiment more often and come up with new workout programs fairly frequently.

> **Using the super routines of the super stars will allow you to skip a lot of wasted time on routines that are not very productive.**

Some champions such as Dorian Yates and Porter Cottrell specialize in training research. You have the benefit of the best of the champion's discoveries by using the super routines of the super stars, the routines that have been proven to work. *Super Routines of the Super Stars* allows you to skip all of the mediocre workouts that are not as productive.

Pushing Past Presuppositions

You may have certain presuppositions that tell you a certain training style won't work. However, if a champion has used it successfully, it must have some merit – and perhaps you should give it a go. So don't dismiss any cycle without at least giving it a short audition in your routine rotation. You might be surprised by something you didn't think would work!

Workout Menu

You can use *Super Routines of the Super Stars* like a menu to choose from. Some people have a hard time coming up with anything more than a basic training routine and this book will give you a much wider selection to choose from. The various cycles will also stimulate new workout cycles for you as you add or blend the cycles to your current training approach, or radically change your training approach and go with something

Jason Arntz

Don Long

The Adjustment Factor

In order to make a cycle work for you, you may have to make some adjustments to the champion's listed cycle. Most often this involves the amount of weight used. If you try and crank up the iron at the same heavy weight as the champion, you may injure yourself. So adjust the weights to your current level of strength. And don't worry about it – just incrementally increase the weights as you get stronger. And you will get stronger.

The number of exercises, sets or repetitions may also have to be adjusted down in the initial stages also. To say that you can step up to the level of a world champion in one instant is false – you have to put in your dues, too.

Roland Cziurlok

totally different. Whatever approach you choose, let *Super Routines of the Super Stars* provide you with some fuel for "hot" new workouts.

Super Routines of the Super Stars can be a great reference book, a tool you can use for continually stimulating workouts. Don't get stuck on one cycle for life – try something new. It is often when we step out into the new and unknown that we make some beneficial discoveries.

To say that you can step up to the level of a world champion in an instant is false – you have to pay your dues first.

Jean-Pierre Fux

Slowly build up your strength. Take your time, do it right – we'll get you there! Use the champion's routine, but modify it somewhat. If he performs 5 sets of a certain type of exercise, you might start with 3 or 4 sets. And if he performs five different exercises for his chest, you might want to start with three. Use this routine as a guide. Gradually work your way toward his workout scheme. As you do, your muscles will become larger and stronger.

The Formula

No cycle will do you any good unless you put in some red-hot intensity in the gym. Successfully transforming your body into mounds of muscle comes from a combination of key factors, not just one single element. The factors that make it happen are knowledge, desire, dedication, and intense application of iron. *Super Routines of the Super Stars* provides the knowledge, the information and insight from the best bodybuilders.

You have to come up with the other primary factors – desire, dedication, and intense application of iron. You have to have a deep desire to change your body into the shape you want it to be. And you have to be dedicated to that end – a short-term desire will take you nowhere. Consistency is king in the gym. And that is where you have to put it all to work – in the gym.

Consistency is king in the gym.

Head knowledge is no good without strong action. You have to put what you know to work – make the body feel what the mind knows. If you can do that, then you will go places with your physique. You will really radically change the shape and condition of your body. *Super Routines of the Super Stars* will give you direction on how to get there quicker.

1) Glenn Bland, *Success! The Glenn Bland Method* (Wheaton: Tyndale House, 1987), 44.

Paul Dillett

SUPER ROUTINES OF THE SUPER STARS - Hot Training Cycles for Ultimate Muscle Growth!

CHAPTER TWO

Total-body Cycles

a total-body training cycle as listed in this chapter, or make your own by combining several of the individual bodypart cycles that are listed in the following chapters.

When you see a total-body training cycle, as opposed to just individual bodyparts, you get the advantage of seeing how the champion puts the full program together, including the rotation of the training days. This gives you a better idea of how the program fits together and what you will have to do. Copy the program or modify it slightly to suit your style. Some champion bodybuilders use a variety of training cycles as they prepare for a contest. Others use the same basic weight-training approach but vary their diet and cardiovascular training as a contest approach. A variety of total-body routines will be presented so you get a good idea of how a full program works.

Roland Cziurlok

> *Some champion bodybuilders use a variety of training cycles as they prepare for a contest.*

Once you have seen how a full-body training cycle is constructed and used by a champion bodybuilder the choice as to the next step is up to you. You can use a similar cycle by slightly modifying the champion's or by using the champion's cycle as a general guide for setting up a similar structure with a few different exercises, or you can use the exact same cycle as the champion.

Time

Give the cycle some time to work. It takes a couple of months for noticeable changes to begin to take place in most any routine so don't abandon any cycle too soon. Give the body time to build up and then determine if this cycle is working for you. Give a cycle at least a couple of months' time to discover if it is effective for you or not as effective as you want. And remember that it is often the effort that you put into the cycle that will make or break the success of that cycle.

There are many different types of training cycles. In the following chapters the super routines of the super stars will be presented by bodypart (muscle group). In this chapter the total-body training cycle will be presented.

Complete Package

The total-body cycle is a complete training package. It encompasses the full spectrum of the weight-training program in a bodybuilding routine. You can choose to use

> Give a cycle at least a couple of months' time to discover if it is effective for you or not as effective as you want.

Arnold Schwarzenegger

Arnold's total-body package was the key to his overall success. Here Franco Columbu helps him work his chest.

Arnold Schwarzenegger's Six-day Superset Program [1]

Monday and Thursday program
Thighs, calves, waist

Squats and leg curls superset together
5 sets of 10 repetitions
Leg extensions and lunges superset together
10 sets of 15 repetitions
Standing calf raises and situps superset together
5 sets of 15 repetitions
Leg raises and sitting calf raises superset together
5 sets of 15 repetitions
Twists and wrist curls

Tuesday and Friday
Back, chest, and shoulders

Bench presses and chinups superset together
5 sets of 15 repetitions
Barbell incline presses and wide-grip barbell rowing superset together

The following pages contain several total-body training cycles from the champions. Choose and use the ones that you want to. Make modifications where and when necessary.

5 sets of 12 to 15 repetitions
Dumbell flyes and T-bar rowing superset together
5 sets of 10 to 12 repetitions
Pullovers
5 sets of 15 repetitions
Presses behind the neck and lateral raises superset together
5 sets of 10 to 12 repetitions
Bent-over lateral raises and wrist curls superset together
5 sets of 15 repetitions
Calf raises and situps
5 sets of 15 repetitions of calf raises
5 sets of 50 repetitions of situps

Wednesday and Saturday Program
Arms
Triceps cable pulldowns and dumbell curls on incline bench superset together
5 sets of 10 to 12 repetitions
Dumbell triceps extensions and preacher-bench curls superset together
5 sets of 15 repetitions
Lying triceps presses with bar and concentration curls superset together
5 sets of 15 repetitions
Reverse curls and wrist curls superset together
5 sets of 15 repetitions
Also on Wednesdays and Saturdays
accelerate your calf and waist-training

Arnold's superset program is definitely not for the faint-hearted! A lot of sets and repetitions. This superset cycle from Arnold is a progressive routine. It allows you to fully work the body twice a week. There are several supersets involved with each workout, so maybe it would be best to start with three sets per exercise instead of five and work up to the level that Arnold prescribes.

Lee Haney's Massive Muscle-building Cycle [2]

"My training routine is usually three days on, one day off; sometimes three on, two off. The degree of intensity I put into a workout determines the frequency of my training."

Day One – Chest, biceps, and triceps.
Day Two – Quads in the morning, hamstrings in the evening.
Day Three – Back in the morning, shoulders in the evening. On the fourth day, I may train my lower back. Calves are trained every other day.
Chest – Bench presses (warmup, then progressively heavier).
Legs – Leg presses and squats.
Back – Barbell rows, T-bar rows, cable pulldowns and cable rows

Lee's arms are only one reason he is the longest-standing Mr. Olympia. You need a total package to be the best in the world.

Lee Haney

Lee Haney

Dorian Yates' "Mr. Olympia" ₃Training Cycle

Day One

Shoulders, triceps, abs

Dumbell presses
2 warmup sets; 1 set of 6 to 8 repetitions
Smith machine behind-the-neck presses
2 warmup sets; 1 set of 6 to 8 repetitions
Standing lateral raises
1 triple-drop set of 5, 5, 5 repetitions
Cable lateral raises
1 set of 6 to 8 repetitions
Nautilus triceps extensions
2 warmup sets; 1 set of 6 to 8 repetitions
Pushdowns
1 set of 6 to 8 repetitions
Reverse crunches (superset)
3 sets of 12 to 15 repetitions
Crunches
3 sets of 12 to 15 repetitions

Day Two

Back and rear delts

Nautilus plate-loaded
2 warmup sets
Pullovers
1 set of 5 to 8 repetitions
Reverse-grip pulldowns
1 set of 5 to 8 repetitions
Chinups
1 set of 5 to 8 repetitions
Yates row (this is similar to the reverse-grip bent-over row)
1 warmup set; 1 set of 5 to 8 repetitions

Biceps – Barbell and dumbell curls (warmup and then four heavy sets of each) followed by EZ-bar preacher curls, followed by slow cable curls or dumbell concentration curls.

Triceps – cable pushdowns for five sets, then lying or standing French presses and reverse triceps dumbell extensions or triceps kickbacks, or triceps pushups on a bench.

Shoulders – Presses behind the neck, warm-up and four sets. Alternate dumbell presses, side laterals, rear laterals, and upright rows from behind.

The repetition range suggested by Lee is 5 to 7 repetitions for the power movements (the main movements in this routine) and up to 12 repetitions for the rhythmic movements (the supporting movements). He uses one warmup set and 3 to 4 heavy sets, and he also stretches each bodypart after every set.

Lee notes that "where most bodybuilders stop the power movements when they get ready for a contest, I stay with them. My reps stay the same, because it's still important for me to train for as much size as possible." Lee's power workout cycle does not contain as many sets or exercises per bodypart as does Arnold's superset routine. The lower set and repetition range allows for the use of heavier weights and this tends to build more muscle mass.

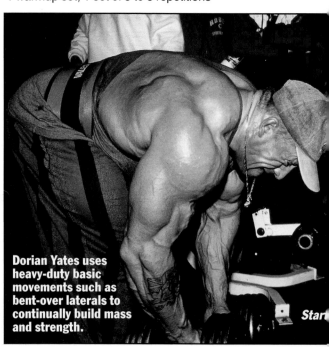

Dorian Yates uses heavy-duty basic movements such as bent-over laterals to continually build mass and strength.

Start

Hammer rows
1 set of 5 to 8 repetitions
Seated cable rows
1 set of 5 to 8 repetitions
Bent-over laterals
1 set of 5 to 8 repetitions
Barbell shrugs
1 set of 5 to 8 repetitions
Back extensions
1 set of 10 to 12 repetitions
Deadlifts
1 set of 5 to 8 repetitions

Day Three – rest and recuperation

Day Four

Chest and biceps

Smith-machine incline presses
3 warmup sets; 1 set of 6 to 8 repetitions
Dumbell incline presses
1 set of 6 to 8 repetitions
Dumbell flyes
warmup set; 1 triple-drop set of 6, 6, 6 repetitions
Seated incline dumbell curls
1 set of 6 to 8 repetitions
Concentration curls
1 set of 6 to 8 repetitions
Barbell curls
1 set of 6 to 8 repetitions
Hammer curls
1 set of 6 to 8 repetitions

Day Five – rest and recuperation

Day Six

Upper and lower legs

Leg extensions
3 warmup sets; 1 set of 8 to 10 repetitions

Mr. Olympia
Dorian Yates.

Leg presses
1 warmup set; 1 set of 8 to 10 repetitions
Smith-machine squats
1 warmup set; 1 set of 8 to 10 repetitions
Hack squats
1 set of 8 to 10 repetitions
Lying leg curls
1 set of 5 to 8 repetitions
Seated leg curls
1 set of 5 to 8 repetitions
Standing leg curls
1 set of 5 to 8 repetitions
Stiff-leg deadlifts
1 set of 8 to 10 repetitions
Standing calf raises
1 set of 12 to 15 repetitions
Seated calf raises
1 set of 12 to 15 repetitions

Dorian points out that he follows a basic routine, using forced reps, drop sets and other intensity-producing techniques to take the muscle well past the point of failure. He starts his precontest preparation cycle three and a half months

Finish

Porter Cottrell and the late Andreas Munzer.

before the contest, increasing his aerobic work as the contest approaches (changing from three workouts a week of 30 minutes to six workouts of one hour) and reducing his caloric intake.

Dorian's workout is heavy duty and high intensity, in the style of Mike Mentzer's revolutionary approach. Dorian's training cycle utilizes fewer sets than most styles of training. The difference is that Dorian squeezes every possible amount of effort out of the one or two sets that he performs. And his style of a training cycle works – he is undefeated in the past five Mr. Olympia contests. One of the advantages of Dorian's style of training is that a lot more time is allowed for rest and recuperation. This helps the body grow bigger and stronger because it removes the problem of overtraining.

Overtraining is a serious setback to any attempts to gain muscle mass and is a mistake that many make. Dorian's training cycle is put together so that it avoids this problem, thus letting the muscular gains continue for long periods of time.

How can you make Dorian's training cycle work for you? One of the most important factors is intensity. If you try Dorian's shorter training cycle and don't go all-out with 100 percent effort, then you will not obtain the results you want. If you are going to use a short and heavy-duty training approach like Dorian's, you have to get intense and really push each set to the maximum. You have to

totally focus on each muscle group you are working and learn to put all of your effort into just one or two sets instead of four or five as with the traditional workout.

Porter Cottrell's Mass Cycle [4]

Day 1
Chest

Bench presses	4 sets of 15 repetitions
Incline presses	4 sets of 15 repetitions
Incline flyes	4 sets of 8 to 12 repetitions

Delts

Dumbell presses	4 sets of 15 repetitions
Lateral raises	4 sets of 8 to 15 repetitions
Bent-over laterals	4 sets of 8 to 15 repetitions
Dumbell shrugs	4 sets of 12 repetitions

Day 2
Back

Lat pulldowns	4 sets of 12 repetitions
Barbell rows	4 sets of 6 to 15 repetitions
One-arm dumbell rows	4 set of 10 to 20 repetitions

Biceps

Barbell curls	4 sets of 6 to 12 repetitions
Alternate dumbell curls	4 sets of 6 to 15 repetitions
Cable preacher curls	4 sets of 15 to 20 repetitions

Day 3 is for rest and recuperation

Bent-over laterals

Start (left image)

Finish (right image)

When developed, as Porter Cottrell's are, smaller muscle groups such as shoulders elevate a well-developed physique to a higher level.

Day 4
Triceps

Pushdowns	6 sets of 8 to 20 repetitions
Lying extensions	4 sets of 8 to 15 repetitions
Reverse-grip pushdowns	2 sets of 8 to 15 repetitions

Legs

Leg extensions	4 sets of 10 to 20 repetitions
Squats	4 sets of 15 repetitions
Seated leg curls	4 sets of 8 to 15 repetitions
Lying leg curls	4 sets of 8 to 10 repetitions

"In training, I've found out that a two-day-on, one-day-off training schedule works best for building mass," says Porter. "Taking a rest day after every two days really helps to boost recovery ability. Further, I think if you can implement that into your schedule, (i.e. training two bodyparts each day, such as chest and shoulders one day, back and biceps the next) that's all you need to stimulate maximum growth. Maintaining strict form is imperative. I never cheat on my movements and I'm very strict in their execution." Porter Cottrell's training cycle for mass is a well-balanced training approach. There is a good amount of rest allowed

Dumbell shrugs

Start (left image)

Finish (right image)

yet each bodypart gets full stimulation from weekly training. Porter uses a steady 4 sets per bodypart. He uses a fairly high repetition range. When many repetitions are performed in fairly strict and slow motion the muscles really get stimulated.

Porter's mass-building routine is different than Lee Haney's (Lee uses lower repetitions) in some aspects yet similar in others. Both use about 4 sets per bodypart.

Craig Titus' Split Cycle [5]

Craig splits his body over four days but trains two days on/one day off. That rest every third day helps with both recovery and growth.

Day 1 (a.m.) chest (p.m.) biceps
Day 2 (a.m.) back (p.m.) hamstrings
Day 3 rest
Day 4 (a.m.) shoulders (p.m.) triceps
Day 5 quads

Calves and abs are done every other day.

Craig is a believer in high sets for a muscle. He normally does four or five exercises per muscle group, with each exercise getting 4 sets. He starts with a weight he can handle for 12 repetitions the first set. Each succeeding set he drops the reps by one; thus his sets are always 12, 11, 10 and 9 reps. Some exercises he pyramids up in weight as the reps drop. Other times he uses the same weight each set and just drops the reps.

Craig rotates the workout around to allow for some rest because he uses heavy poundages. Craig uses a twice-a-day split for his training cycle. This is a great way to enable yourself to spend more time on each muscle group. If you are training just one muscle group per workout, then you can really concentrate and focus on that muscle group and give it exclusive attention. The single-exercise-per-workout cycle is a good way to promote fast growth. This single muscle group workout also allows your workout to be shorter in length.

Craig's cycle is similar to some of the other cycles in that he works out for a couple of days, then takes a rest day before a third workout. He also uses four or five exercises with a higher set and repetition count, which is fairly similar to what some of the other champions use.

Craig Titus' cycle allows him to focus clearly on whichever muscle he is working.

Start

Pulldowns to the front

Finish

Jeff Long's Total Body-training Cycle [6]

Monday
Back
Tuesday
Chest
Wednesday
Rest
Thursday
Legs
Friday
Arms and shoulders
Saturday
Rest

For the back workout, Jeff (NPC middleweight champion) uses bent-over rows, pulldowns to the front, T-bar rows, low-pulley seated cable rows and high-cable close-grip pulldowns. He uses 4 sets of 10 to 15 repetitions per exercise.

His chest workout consists of incline-bench presses, flat-bench presses, and flyes. He uses heavy weights for 10 to 12 repetitions.

Leg-training consists of leg extensions, squats, leg presses, hack squats, lying leg curls, standing leg curls and walking lunges. For the leg exercises he performs 20 repetitions per set for 3 or 4 sets!

> Overtraining is a serious setback to any attempts to gain muscle mass and is a mistake that many make.

Sonny Schmidt

His arms are trained with pushdowns, dumbell kickbacks and close-grip bench presses for the triceps. He performs 4 sets of 12 to 15 repetitions. The biceps are stimulated with EZ-curls, alternating standing dumbell curls, and incline dumbell curls for 4 sets of 12 to 15 repetitions. Jeff trains his shoulders with dumbell laterals, upright rows, front laterals, shoulder shrugs, and bent-over laterals.

He trains five days out of seven, using high repetitions and giantsets (four sets of different exercises performed back-to-back without rest. He says, "Giantsets increase your intensity of training without increasing the amount of time you train. You try to cram more work into that same period of exercise time."

Jeff's workout is another cycle style that is not for the faint-hearted. Giantsets are about as tough as it gets.

Sonny Schmidt's Super Routine [7]
Day One – A.M.
Chest
Bench presses
6 sets of 10 to 12 repetitions
Incline presses
4 sets of 10 to 12 repetitions
Dumbell flyes
4 sets of 8 to 10 repetitions

Start

Sonny Schmidt uses lots of sets, reps and exercises in his cycle. Here he demonstrates triceps pushdowns.

Finish

Cable crossovers
4 sets of 15 to 20 repetitions
Biceps
Barbell curls
5 sets of 10 to 15 repetitions
Preacher curls
5 sets of 10 to 15 repetitions
Concentration curls
5 sets of 10 to 15 repetitions
Wrist curls
5 sets of 15 to 20 repetitions
P.M.
Back
Front pulldowns
5 sets of 10 to 12 repetitions
Behind-the-neck pulldowns
5 sets of 10 to 12 repetitions
Seated cable rows
4 sets of 10 to 12 repetitions
T-bar rows
4 sets of 10 to 12 repetitions
Day 2 – A.M.
Shoulders
Barbell overhead presses

6 sets of 8 to 10 repetitions
Lateral raises
4 sets of 15 repetitions
Bent-over lateral raises
4 sets of 15 repetitions
Dumbell presses
4 sets of 10 repetitions
P.M.
Calves, Hamstrings
Standing calf raises
8 sets of 15 to 20 repetitions
Seated calf raises
8 sets of 15 to 20 repetitions
Stiff-leg deadlifts
5 sets of 15 to 20 repetitions
Lying leg curls
5 sets of 15 to 20 repetitions
Day 3 – A.M.
Quads
Squats
6 sets of 10 to 15 repetitions
Leg extensions
4 sets of 20 to 50 repetitions
Leg presses
4 sets of 10 to 15 repetitions
Hack squats
4 sets of 10 to 15 repetitions
P.M.
Triceps
Lying triceps extensions
5 sets of 10 to 15 repetitions
Pushdowns
5 sets of 10 to 15 repetitions
One-arm cable pushdowns
5 sets of 10 to 15 repetitions

Sonny takes two minutes of rest between sets, particularly after heavy sets. "My philosophy is that if resting another minute or two allows me to handle 25 percent more weight, then *#%*#, I'd be a fool not to. Too many beginners sacrifice growth-inducing poundages by rushing to do another set before the muscle is fully recovered." Sonny uses lots of sets, repetitions and exercises in his training cycle to achieve his objectives. Sonny's training cycle is a tough one – he performs it six days a week, with only a day off, and he uses a double split! But it is very effective for him as it allowed him to win the Masters Olympia title at the age of 42.

Football Firepower

How do those big football players get so powerful and massive? They use a power weight-training program. They use a cycle that bulks them up with massive muscle size. Want an example? How about All-Pro Chad Hennings, formerly of the world champion Dallas

Cowboys and now of the Miami Dolphins. Chad is 6'5", 292 pounds, bench presses 500 pounds, squats 610 pounds and runs the 40-yard dash in 4.75 seconds. What does his weight-training cycle look like?

Huge Chad Hennings' Super Cycle[8]

Monday
Upper body (light)
Dumbell bench presses
3 sets of 8 repetitions
Pullups
3 sets of 8 repetitions
Dumbell shoulder presses
3 sets of 10 repetitions
Neck machine
2 sets of 8 to 12 repetitions
External and internal rotation with dumbells
3 sets of 10 repetitions
Dumbell flyes
3 sets of 8 repetitions
Crunches
3 sets of 25 repetitions

Tuesday
Lower body
Squats
3 sets of 10, 8 and 8 repetitions
Leg extensions
2 sets of 8 to 12 repetitions
Leg curls
2 sets of 8 to 12 repetitions
Abductor/adductor machine
2 sets of 15 to 20 repetitions
Calf raises
2 sets of 15 to 20 repetitions
Lower-back machine
2 sets of 15 repetitions

Thursday
Upper body (heavy)
Bench presses
3 sets of 8, 5 and 5 repetitions
Behind-the-neck pulldowns
3 sets of 10 repetitions
21s on cables
1 set of 21 repetitions
Dumbell shrugs
3 sets of 8 to 10 repetitions
Neck machine
2 sets of 8 to 12 repetitions
External and internal rotation
3 sets of 10 repetitions
Pec-dek
2 sets of 8 to 10 repetitions
Crunches
3 sets of 25 repetitions

Although Chad Hennings' cycle is designed for explosive power for use in football, there are some similarities to a bodybuilding schedule. A rotation of a heavy and light schedule for the upper body, and taking some time off for

Lee Labrada blasts his calves with donkey calf raises.

Finish

Start

Vary all aspects of your routine to target more effectively and avoid overtraining.

recovery are similar to many bodybuilding cycles. The training is well placed to cover the muscle groups and yet avoid overtraining.

Lee Labrada's Periodization Cycle [9]

Day One
Chest, shoulders, and triceps
Day Two
Back, biceps, and abdominals
Day Three
Rest and recuperation
Day Four
Quads, hams, and calves

Lee uses his cycle in three phases – an activation phase of high repetitions (12 to 15) using less weight for four or five exercises per bodypart. After three weeks he moves into a strength phase of heavy weight training with only 4 to 6 repetitions and only three exercises per bodypart. The final phase is a mass phase, where he uses medium-heavy weight for 8 to 10 repetitions for up to four exercises per bodypart. For each phase, he uses 3 or 4 sets of each exercise. Lee structures his workout to avoid overtraining. He points out that "traditional routines, where you work more than two days in a row, really cut into your recuperation period. This six-day training stuff? Forget it, man. Guys who use that style of training make gains for maybe a year, and then are finished. I've gone through the whole gamut, from six days a week to five, to three on/one off. I've tried everything, but the routine I'm using now works the best. It gives my body time to recover, especially if I want growth."

Lee's routine is moving in the same direction that many of the bodybuilding champions are headed – less weekly workouts, and more time for rest and recuperation. Lee has taken it a step further by breaking the cycle down into three distinct phases and this is working well for him. His style of training (the intelligent approach) is the wave of the future.

Flex Wheeler's No Cease-fire Cycle [10]

Flex Wheeler has climbed to the top echelon of the physique world. What type of training did he use to get to this position? An example of his training style is the cycle he used before the Nationals.
Back
Pulldowns to the rear – 6 sets, up to 270 pounds.
One-arm cable rows – 5 sets
Seated cable rows using high pulley – 5 sets
Pulldowns to the front – 5 sets
One-arm rows from cable pulley – 5 sets
Barbell shrugs – 5 sets, up to 405 pounds.
Arms
Triceps pushdowns using V-handle – 6 sets
Single-arm pushdowns – 6 sets
Single-arm pushdowns with twist – 6 sets
Dumbell curls – 5 sets
Hammer curls – 5 sets
Preacher concentration curls with EZ-curl bar – 5 sets

Lee Labrada and Flex Wheeler compare abdominals.

Cable crossovers
Start

Finish

Flex Wheeler's training cycle has given him the physique needed to seize success in the bodybuilding world.

One-arm concentration cable curls – 5 sets

Chest

Bench presses – 6 sets, up to 355 pounds.
Incline dumbell presses
– 5 sets, up to 130 pounds.
Flyes – 5 sets, up to 80 pounds.
Cable flyes on incline bench – 5 sets
Cable flyes on flat bench – 5 sets
Cable crossovers – 5 sets

Shoulders

Bent-over lateral raises – 5 sets
Standing lateral raises – 5 sets
Dumbell front raises – 5 sets

Legs

Single leg curls – 6 sets
Leg curls – 6 sets

Seated leg curls – 6 sets
Leg extensions – 5 sets
Leg raises to side with cable attached – 5 sets
Frog squats – 5 sets
Hack squats – 5 sets

Abdominals

Cable crunches from high pulley – 6 sets

Calves

Seated calf raises – 6 sets
Calf raises on leg-press machine – 6 sets
Standing or donkey calf raises – 6 sets
The repetition range is from 8 to 12 on all exercises

Flex trains his body in three days, combining back and arms on day one, chest and shoulders (along with traps) on day two, and legs and calves on day three.

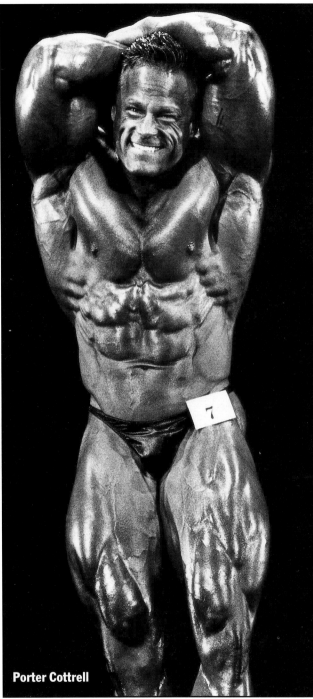

Porter Cottrell

Another From the Oak

How about having a champion prescribe a training cycle for a person at an intermediate level? And what if the champion was Arnold? In his book, *Arnold: The Education of a Bodybuilder*, there is an intermediate training cycle prescribed by the Oak:

Monday and Thursday
Legs
Squats – 5 sets of 8 repetitions
Leg extensions – 5 sets of 12 repetitions
Leg curls – 5 sets of 8 to 10 repetitions
Standing calf raises – 5 sets of 15 repetitions
Chest
Bench presses – 5 sets of 8 to 15 repetitions
Flyes – 5 sets of 10 repetitions
Abdomen and Forearms
Bent-knee situps – 200 repetitions during the day
Bent-knee leg raises – 200 repetitions during the day
Wrist curls – 5 sets of 15 repetitions
Tuesday and Friday
Shoulders
Presses behind the neck – 5 sets of 8 repetitions
Lateral raises – 5 sets of 8 to 10 repetitions
Back
Behind-the-neck chinups – 6 sets of 10 repetitions
Bent-over rows – 5 sets of 12 repetitions
Arms
Barbell curls – 2 sets of 8 and 3 sets of 6
Seated dumbell curls – 5 sets of 8 repetitions
Restricted incline curls – 5 sets of 10 repetitions
Standing French presses – 5 sets of 12 repetitions
Lying triceps extensions – 5 sets of 10 to 12 repetitions
Abdomen and forearm work
Wednesday – work on your weak points.

Not all champions use the same training philosophy. If you are astute, you can see what is similar and dissimilar in the various routines.

Use this chapter to help you set up your training cycle. As mentioned earlier, you do not have to do everything exactly the same as the champions (indeed, it would be a good idea to start out at a reduced level) but you can learn the routine rhythm that the champions have in the way they use a cycle. Use *Super Routines of the Super Stars* as both a guide and motivation for your own training.

1) Arnold Schwarzenegger and Douglas Kent Hall, *Arnold: The Education of a Bodybuilder* (New York: Pocket Books, 1977), 247-254.

2) Lee Haney, "Big, Bigger, Biggest," *Flex* (August 1990), 44.

3) Bill Geiger, "How I Won the Mr. Olympia," *Muscle & Fitness* (January 1996), 76.

4) Porter Cottrell, "How to Gain 10 Pounds of Muscle," *Muscle & Fitness* (October 1994), 142.

5) Greg Zulak, "Titanic Delts & Traps," *MuscleMag International* (August 1994), 36.

6) Reg Bradford, "Super-Size Total Body Workout," *Muscular Development* (March 1996), 122.

7) Marty Gallagher, "How He Won the Master's Olympia" *Muscle & Fitness* (January 1996), 86.

8) Jim Rosenthal, "The Cowboy Way to Building Power, Strength, & Stamina," *Muscle & Fitness* (October 1993), 148.

9) T.C. Luoma, "Periodization Training" *MuscleMag International* (October 1993), 94.

10) Gayle Hall, "Ken 'Flex' Wheeler Flexes His Way to the Gold," *MuscleMag International* (February 1990), 42.

Flex Wheeler

Shawn Ray

SUPER ROUTINES OF THE SUPER STARS - Hot Training Cycles for Ultimate Muscle Growth!

CHAPTER THREE

Turbocharged Torso-training Cycles

additional ideas for training your torso at a higher level, read on. This chapter contains the torso-training cycles of many super star bodybuilders. These routines are turbocharged, high-powered stuff!

The champions have to really blast their torsos to force the massive and shapely muscle that wins contests and stands out in a crowd. Find out what these training cycles are in the following pages.

Routine Rotation

The training cycles in this chapter are different than the last in that the focus is on a single bodypart instead of the full body. This allows you to rotate or mix training cycle workouts. You might choose to try something like Dorian Yates' back-training cycle and Kevin Levrone's shoulder workout. You have more options than with the total-body training cycle. And you can put together a more precise training cycle by picking and choosing different styles for different bodyparts.

Don't get stuck on just one training style!

Check out each of the different torso-training cycles of the different champions. Remember, the star body-builders often vary their training cycle

Vince Taylor

Training the torso is tough work but it yields the rugged muscularity on the frame of the body that looks so fantastic. The groups of the chest, back, and shoulders combine to make up a large amount of muscle mass provided that you have trained this area correctly. If you are quite sure that you know how, or would like some

and training routine so what they may have done in one phase or year of training may be different than in another year or phase. Cycles vary and it is good to get a large overview of the various types. This chapter of *Super Routines of the Super Stars* provides a good overview of various training cycles, with emphasis on the torso region.

Dorian Yates

Weighted hyperextensions –
1 set of 8 to 12 repetitions
Deadlifts – 1 set of 6 to 8 repetitions

Dorian performs each single set after a warmup of 1 or 2 sets for most exercises. Dorian utilizes a close grip for his lat work instead of the traditional wide grip because he believes that it works the lat muscles further down the back, toward the point of insertion. Dorian points out that his emphasis is not so much on lifting the weight but on achieving a fuller range of motion. To do this he makes certain that his form is superstrict.

What if Dorian were to set up a back-training routine for someone who was not quite as advanced as he was? How do you think such a routine might be put together? You don't need to guess anymore. He has put together a back routine for those who are just getting into working out. It looks like this:

Close-grip lat pulldowns (with curl grip) – 3 sets of 8 to 10 repetitions
Barbell rows – 3 sets of 8 to 10 repetitions
Deadlifts – 3 sets of 6 to 8 repetitions

Dorian advises those who use this routine to perform it twice a week, consistently, and the back will grow. He points out that lat pulldowns add size and width to the lats and barbell rows add strength and thickness to the whole back.

Dorian's Devastating[1,2] Back Cycle

What better way to start than with the best in the business? Dorian's back routine is superintense and quite comprehensive.

Nautilus pullovers –
1 set of 6 to 8 repetitions
Reverse-grip pulldowns –
1 set of 6 to 8 repetitions
Barbell rows –
1 set of 6 to 8 repetitions
One-arm hammer machine rows –
1 set of 6 to 8 repetitions
Cable rows –
1 set of 6 to 8 repetitions
Rear-delt machine –
1 set of 6 to 8 repetitions

Start

Finish

Dorian Yates trains superheavy using rows to add strength and thickness to his whole back.

Robby Robinson's Chest Cycle[3]

Incline-bench presses
Vertical-bench presses
Pec-dek
Cable crossovers

Robby performs either 4 sets of 10 to 12 repetitions or on a heavy day he will warm up with 12 to 15 repetitions and then go to three sets of five repetitions with a heavy weight.

Robby points out – "I'm very careful to keep the mind-muscle link in place for every rep, especially toward the end of the set. The emphasis, as always, is on keeping tension on the muscle at all times."

Nasser's Nasty Deltoid Routine[4]

Nasser El Sonbaty is the star on the rise. At 5'11" and 270+ pounds, he is a powerful package of muscle. He pushed Dorian Yates to

Robby Robinson

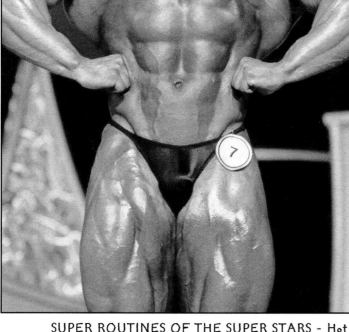

Nasser El Sonbaty

the wall in the last Mr. Olympia. Nasser has a thick and muscular torso, capped off with some heavy-duty deltoids. One of his deltoid cycles is as follows:

Seated lateral raises
 1 set of 12 repetitions with 25 pounds
 1 set of 12 repetitions with 35 pounds
 1 set of 8 repetitions with 50 pounds
 1 set of 8 repetitions with 60 pounds
Rear-delt machine
 3 sets of 10 to 15 repetitions with the stack
 1 set of 10 to 15 repetitions with the stack
Seated dumbell presses
 1 set of 12 repetitions with 75 pounds
 1 set of 10 repetitions with 110 pounds
 1 set of 8 repetitions with 140 pounds
 1 set of 8 repetitions with 160 pounds
Nasser's last two reps for each group are forced reps.

Lee Labrada

Lee Labrada's Back Program for Beginning, Intermediate and Advanced Stages of Training.[5]

Lee Labrada is a bodybuilder with a great back. Here he provides advice on three types of back routines (beginner, intermediate, and advanced).

Beginner:
Bent-over rows – 3 or 4 sets of 8 to 10 repetitions
Pullups – 3 or 4 sets of as many repetitions as possible

Lee suggests you "work on form first and foremost, but gaining strength and using more weight to progressively stress the muscles will keep you growing. Hold the peak contraction and learn to contract the back muscles properly."

Intermediate:
Pullups or pulldowns – 3 sets of 8 to 10 repetitions
Bent-over rows or one-arm dumbell rows –
3 sets of 8 to 10 repetitions
Back extensions or deadlifts –
3 sets of 10 to 15 repetitions
Shrugs – 3 sets of 8 to 10 repetitions

Lee points out that at the intermediate level you want to get stronger but not at the expense of form. He urges the intermediate trainee to keep the intensity level high.

Advanced:
Pullups or underhand-grip pulldowns –
3 sets of 10 repetitions

Never sacrifice form for strength but still keep your intensity level as high as possible.

Bent-over rows

Start

Finish

One-arm
dumbell
rows
Start

Finish

One-arm dumbell rows – four sets of 9 to 12 repetitions
Close-grip pulldowns to the front –
four sets of 9 to 12 repetitions
Machine seated rows – four sets of 9 to 12 repetitions

After Craig performs his back workout he notes that he's done. "I'm just totally drained. If you do a hard back workout properly you shouldn't have the energy to do anything more."

Kevin Levrone's Shoulder Cycle [7]

Kevin has what are probably the most awesome shoulders in bodybuilding and they helped him almost topple Dorian Yates in the 1995 Mr. Olympia. Here is one of his shoulder-training routines.

Dumbell presses – 4 sets of 12 repetitions

Craig Titus

Increase the weight and decrease the reps as you progress through your workout.

One-arm cable rows –
3 sets of 10 repetitions
Bent-over rows – 3 sets of 10 repetitions
Back extensions or deadlifts –
3 sets of 10 to 20 repetitions
Dumbell shrugs –
3 sets of 10 to 12 repetitions

Lee notes that when training for size the muscles must be progressively fatigued from the time you walk in until the time that you leave. He believes a short, intense workout is much better than a long, drawn-out training session. He says that all four parts of the back should be attacked in this order: lats, middle back, lower back, and traps.

Craig Titus' Back Blast Cycle [6]

Warmup with wide-grip pulldowns to the front – 1 set of 20 to 25 repetitions
Wide-grip pulldowns – four sets of 9 to 12 repetitions. (Use higher repetitions with lighter weights first, lower repetitions with heavier weights next.)
Seated cable rows – four sets of 9 to 12 repetitions, same weight throughout.

Kevin Levrone

Pullups (overhand grip) – 6 sets of 10 repetitions
Barbell prone rows – 4 sets of 10 repetitions
superset with
One-arm dumbell rows – 3 sets of 10 repetitions
Lat machine pulldowns – 6 sets of 10 repetitions (four sets to front; two behind)
Barbell upright rows – 6 sets of 10 repetitions
    This routine was used in preparation for the Mr. America contest, which Val won.

Steve Brisbois' Mr. Universe Back Blowout

Wide-grip chinups
1 set of 12 to 20 repetitions
5 sets of 10 to 12 repetitions
Wide-grip pulldowns
1 set of 20 repetitions
5 or 6 sets of 10 to 12 repetitions
Close-grip pulldowns
1 set of 20 repetitions
5 or 6 sets of 10 to 12 repetitions
Steve uses two of these exercises in any given workout in combination with two of the following
Rope lat pull-ins
1 set of 20 repetitions
5 or 6 sets of 10 to 12 repetitions
One-arm dumbell rows
1 set of 20 repetitions
5 or 6 sets of 10 to 12 repetitions

Seated cable rows

Start

Finish

Train fast and heavy as long as you don't forget to ensure you are feeling the muscle working. – Steve Brisbois

Front raises – 4 sets of 12 repetitions
Single-arm bent-over rear cable raises –
4 sets of 12 repetitions
Standing lateral raises –
4 sets of 12 repetitions
    Kevin uses heavy dumbells for his presses, ranging from 100 to 150 pounds. He uses 50-pound dumbells for the front raises, 40 pounds for the rear raises, and 30 to 40 pounds for the lateral raises. His favorite exercise is the seated dumbell press.

Mr. America Super Back Cycle [8]

Training the torso does not necessarily change that much over the years. Here is a look at the back-training cycle of the 1964 Mr. America, Val Vasilef.

Bent-over rows
1 set of 20 repetitions
5 or 6 sets of 10 to 12 repetitions
T-bar rows
1 set of 20 repetitions
5 to 6 sets of 10 to 12 repetitions
Seated cable rows
1 set of 20 repetitions
5 or 6 sets of 10 to 12 repetitions
To finish off, Steve performs
Shrugs
5 or 6 sets of 10 to 12 repetitions
Deadlifts
5 or 6 sets of 10 to 12 repetitions

Steve uses very heavy weights, but stresses that the "feel" is more important. He also says, "I like to train fast. I seldom rest more than 45 seconds between sets as I don't like to lose the pump and the blood in the muscle. I set a fast tempo and just keep going until the workout is done."

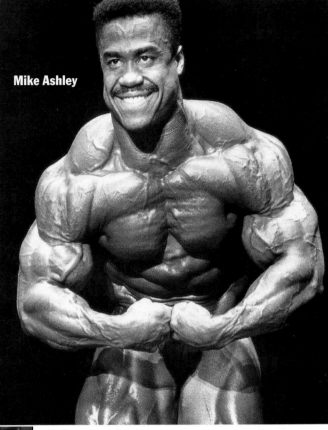

Mike Ashley

Steve Brisbois

Mike Ashley's Chest & Shoulder Cycle[10]

Heavy chest workout:
Barbell bench presses; barbell inclines; occasional declines; pullovers; heavy flyes. 5 or 6 sets per exercise, working up to 3 heavy sets of about 6 reps each.

Medium chest workout:
Switch to dumbells instead of barbells for the flat and incline presses, as well as increasing the repetition range to 10 to 12 on the three hardest sets.

Light chest workout:
Use both barbells and dumbells, but superset many exercises, and increase the repetition range to 12 to 15. A light day means less weight on the bar, but it's very intense. Light doesn't mean easy.

Heavy shoulder workout:
Behind-the-neck presses, barbell upright rows, barbell shrugs. (Again, he completes 5 or 6 sets per exercise beginning with 10 to 12 reps but working up to 3 heavy sets of 6 reps. Sometimes he'll include a higher repetition cooldown set after the three heavy sets.)

Medium shoulder workout:
Dumbell presses, front dumbell raises, rear and lateral raises, cable upright rows.

Ben Weider and
Arnold Schwarzenegger
congratulate a victorious
Michael Francois.

Light shoulder workout:

"My light day is when it gets exciting because it's non-stop. I begin with supinated dumbell presses, then go to cable upright rows, then dumbell front raises and rear and lateral raises. I take no rest with these five exercises. Five rounds of these, and I'm done for the day."

Mike notes that "as well as varying my workouts among heavy, medium, and light weights, I'll cut the overall intensity of everything I do way back at times throughout the year to let my body catch up on the rest it must have to keep performing well."

Michael Francois' Torso Cycle"

Chest
Bench presses:
3 sets to warmup, then 4 sets of 8 repetitions with 3 or 4 forced reps on the 4th set.
High neck incline-bench presses:
3 sets of 8 repetitions with forced reps
Incline dumbell presses:
3 sets of 8 repetitions with forced reps
Hammer bench machine:
3 sets of 8 repetitions with forced reps

Back
Deadlifts:
Power rack, single reps up to 840 pounds at shin level.

Don't plan heavy or light cycles. Work according to how your body feels.

Michael Francois
works his lower
back and
hamstrings with
stiff-leg deadlifts.
Start

Lower the rack pins and work up to 700 pounds on a single rep. Regular deadlift, 3 sets of five repetitions with 400 to 500 pounds.
Shrugs:
4 sets of 12 to 15 repetitions
Cable rows:
3 sets of 8 to 10 repetitions
Wide-grip pulldowns to front
3 sets of 8 to 10 repetitions
Lower-back machine
3 sets of 12 to 20 repetitions

Deltoids
Military presses to front:
Warmup, then 3 sets of 4 to 6 reps, with forced reps.

Shawn Ray

Finish

Dumbell military presses:
3 sets of 8 reps with forced reps
Smith machine presses behind neck:
3 sets of 8 reps
Lateral raises:
3 sets of 12 to 15 repetitions
Rear-delt machine:
3 sets of 12 to 15 repetitions
Mike notes, "I don't plan heavy or light cycles. I just go by my body rhythms. If I feel good, I see no reason to hold back. I will attempt to get eight to ten reps with whatever weight I am using, or until failure occurs. At that point I will have my partner assist me with an additional four reps. This is not a technique I would recommend for anyone but an advanced bodybuilder."

Shawn Ray blasts his back with T-bar rows.
Start

Finish

Shawn Ray's Back Cycle[12]

Seated pulldowns to the front
4 or 5 sets of 10 to 15 repetitions, increasing the weight in 30-pound increments.
Seated cable rows
4 or 5 sets of 12 to 15 reps
T-bar rows
4 or 5 sets of 10 to 15 reps
Chinups to the front
4 sets of 12 reps

Shawn notes, "Chinups can widen your back by working the large outside portion of your lats, and – as Robert Kennedy points out – they widen the shoulder girdle by stretching the scapula. This helps create a V-taper to the upper body. But in order for the exercise to work, good form is essential. Grip the bar firmly. Customarily I'll use a little wider than medium grip, though I will vary from time to time, using close, medium and wide grips. Pull your chest up to the bar – don't yank, and don't swing your body."

Phil Hernon's Heavy-duty Chest Cycle[13]

Decline pushups –
one set to failure (with a 45-pound plate)
Dips – one set of 8 to 10 reps (with two 45-pound plates)
Flat dumbell presses – one set of 10 reps (with 150-pound dumbells)

Start

Don't overlook the benefits of calisthenics such as pushups and dips.
– Phil Hernon

Parillo pec minors (on a dip bar) – one set to failure (Shrug your upper chest and shoulder region with arms locked.)

Phil's workout is very short (it only takes 15 minutes) and very intense. He says you have to work as hard as you can during the workout.

The torso is one of the major regions of the physique and the champion bodybuilders direct a lot of hard work at this region. Use some of the various training approaches from *Super Routines of the Super Stars* to build a torso-training cycle that will work for you. And don't stop at only one cycle – try different styles.

1) Dorian Yates, "Still Growing," *Flex* (May 1996), 112.

2) Dorian Yates, "The Strong and Widening Road," *Flex* (January 1996), 42.

3) Robby Robinson, "Stacked to the Max," *Flex* (March 1996), 90.

4) From "The Beasty Boys Blitz Delts," *Flex* (March 1996), 285.

5) Bill Geiger, "Wings of Victory," *Muscle & Fitness* (August 1995), 91.

6) Greg Zulak, "A Heavyweight Affair," *MuscleMag International* (January 1994), 59.

7) Reg Bradford, "Kevin Levrone's Delt Routine," *MuscleMag International* (January 1994), 29.

8) Robert Kennedy, "Ask Bob," *MuscleMag International* (January 1994), 227.

9) Steve Brisbois, "Back Training Mr. Universe Style," *MuscleMag International* (May, 1988), 29.

10) Gayle Hall, "Mike Ashley, Bittersweet but Tasty Nonetheless," *MuscleMag International* (October 1990), 143.

11) William Brink, "Large and in Charge," *MuscleMag International* (June 1994), 48.

12) Rosemary Hallum, "Blast Your Back Training," *MuscleMag International* (December 1990), 18.

13) Reg Bradford, "Phil Hernon's Chest Training Program," *Muscular Development* (December 1995), 79.

Phil Hernon

Finish

Flex Wheeler

CHAPTER FOUR

Arm-training Cycles

you train your arms, you have to "go hard or go home" for every workout. There is no middle ground in arm-training.

The super stars in the bodybuilding world realize the necessity for hardcore arm-training workouts. You can see the intensity etched into their faces as they train their arms.

Intensity in training the arms is a required ingredient. And so is a good training cycle. What are good arm-training cycles? Several are listed on the following pages. These arm-training cycles have proven successful for the super star bodybuilders and have built the incredible arm size and shape that the champions sport. Take a look at the arm-training super routines of the super stars.

The arms are an area that is both enjoyable and difficult to train. The arms are enjoyable because of the quick and obvious results that occur, and because the arms are a "show" muscle group. However, the arms are also tough to train at times because every arm workout has to be performed at all-out intensity. You might get by with less than a 100 percent effort with some of the other muscle groups but you can't with the arms. A half-hearted arm workout is almost as bad as no arm workout at all. When

"Arm-training has to be intense to be effective."

Milos Sarcev, Ronnie Coleman and Gunter Schlierkamp

Flex Wheeler's "guns" are helping lead his assault on the tops of the pro ranks.

triceps. He trains them once a week. (He uses a five on/one off workout cycle). Flex points out that beginners, intermediates, and hard-gainers may want to try a three on/one off split to target biceps twice a week and that a good beginner's cycle consists of two or three sets of 12 to 15 repetitions for three exercises. Flex also notes that muscle growth occurs not when you lift, but when you recuperate.

Michael Francois' Mass Biceps Cycle [2]

Heavy barbell curls
Heavy dumbell curls

Not a lot of stuff — but effective. Michael writes that "my initial biceps workouts consisted of just heavy barbell and dumbell curls. As a novice bodybuilder, I felt I needed to add more muscle mass, and I knew from my weightlifting experience that the best way to do this was to rely on just a few exercises performed hard and heavy."

Michael advises that for "the optimal number of sets, I'd suggest that a beginner do three exercises for two sets each, or a total of six sets for biceps. The repetitions should be in the 8 to 12 range. When you reach 12 reps for each set, add more weight. Try to push yourself workout after workout, shooting for the 12-rep mark. Such constant progression ensures gains as the muscle accommodates to gradually increasing loads. As a beginner, your primary exercise for biceps should be the barbell curl."

Flex Wheeler's Biceps Cycle [1]

Flex Wheeler is one of the current top guns in the bodybuilding world — and he has the "big guns" to defend his position. He has massive and full biceps that also have a great peak. Here is how he trains them:

EZ-curl barbell curls
3 sets of 10 reps with 100 to 140 pounds

One-arm preacher curls
4 sets of 10 reps with 30 to 45 pounds

Concentration curls
(seated or standing)
3 sets of 10 reps with 35 pounds

Flex trains biceps on the same day that he trains

Steve Davis' Super Arm Cycle [3]

Steve Davis has a cycle he uses for developing the arm size of beginning bodybuilders. It consists of:

Barbell curls
2 sets of 8 repetitions

Incline dumbell curls
2 sets of 8 repetitions

Close grip 2/3 bench presses
2 sets of 8 repetitions
Reverse curls
2 sets of 8 repetitions

This routine is performed twice a week, and is preceded by a couple of sets of behind-the-neck presses, which also work the triceps. Steve advises that three minutes rest should be taken between sets, and that heavy weights should be used.

Skip's Total Arm-training Cycle [4]

Biceps:
Alternate dumbell curls
1 warmup set of 8 to 10 repetitions, 2 sets of 4 to 6 repetitions
Barbell curls
2 sets of 4 to 6 repetitions
Concentration curls
2 sets of 4 to 6 repetitions
Hammer curls
2 sets of 4 to 6 repetitions

Steve Davis

Michael Francois

Triceps:
Dumbell triceps extensions
2 warmup sets of 8 to 12 repetitions
Pushdowns
2 sets of 6 to 8 repetitions
Reverse-grip pushdowns
2 sets of 6 to 8 repetitions
Cable kickbacks
2 sets of 6 to 8 repetitions
Forearms:
Barbell wrist curls
2 sets of 8 to 12 repetitions
Reverse-grip wrist curls
2 sets of 8 to 12 repetitions
Skip LaCour advises training the arms only once a week, and using heavy weights.

If you want to look like a pro, train like a pro.
– Shawn Ray

Shawn's Pro Biceps Cycle [5]

Shawn Ray has biceps that are thick, broad, and high – a full package. He offers biceps-training advice for the beginning and intermediate trainee: If you want arms like the professionals, you should train like the professionals.

Biceps routine:
Standing EZ-bar curls
Standing alternate dumbell curls
Seated alternate dumbell curls
Concentration curls

Shawn advises using three of the four exercises during each workout, and changing the combination regularly. [13] He performs 4 sets of 8 to 12 repetitions for each of these exercises. "Get a full range of motion," Shawn says, "and keep it slow and steady." Shawn focuses on technique and squeezing the biceps during the curl.

Evander's Arm Routine [6]

One of the best-built boxers of all time is Evander Holyfield. And that should be no surprise, since his trainer is Mr. Olympia, Lee Haney. What did Lee advise Evander to do for his arms? How does Evander train his arms? Here is how:

Weighted dips
3 sets of 12 to 15 repetitions
Barbell curls (explosive)
4 sets of 8 repetitions
Angled preacher curls
3 sets of 12 repetitions

Triceps pushdowns
4 sets of 12 repetitions
Lying triceps extensions
3 sets of 8 repetitions

Evander takes his time between sets and also stretches for 15 to 20 minutes before and after each training session.

Paul Dillett's Arm-training Philosophy

Paul Dillett is monstrous – and so are his arms. They push the tape past 23 inches. And he has a philosophy on how to make them even bigger – with instinctive training. He says "to shock my arms, I may train them hard one day and come back the very next day and train them even harder! My arms are so accustomed to me training them on Mondays and Thursdays that they don't expect me to come back the next day and blast them again. The sneak

Shawn Ray

As long as you stay creative your body will never get stale or stop improving.
– Paul Dillett

The massive Paul Dillett.

Lou Ferrigno's Triceps-training Cycle [8]

Lou Ferrigno is another bodybuilder with gigantic arms. He is a bodybuilder who has used almost the same triceps-training cycle for all of his training. He says "believe it or not, I've made almost no changes in my (triceps) program since I began my career."

Triceps pushdowns
Dumbell overhead extensions
Lying triceps extensions
Reverse-grip one-arm pulldowns

Lou does 4 or 5 sets of 10 to 12 repetitions. He points out that form is crucial and that it is important to think about the particular part of the muscle you are working. He says it is important to take each exercise slowly and really squeeze and concentrate on the contraction.

Makkawy's Magic Arms [9]

One bodybuilder with awesome arms is Mohamed Makkawy. He didn't quite win the Mr. Olympia but came very close more than once. He has a tremendous pair of "full" arms. One of his earlier arm-training cycles was:

Close-grip standing barbell curls with EZ-curl bar superset (4 sets) with
Standing EZ-curl bar triceps extensions
Barbell curls superset (4 sets) with
One-arm dumbell triceps extensions

This routine was performed after a shoulder workout. Mohamed performed his repetitions in ultrastrict style with flawless form.

attack forces them to grow. I won't use this sneak attack very often. When I do use it, however, I'll almost immediately notice that my arms stay fuller longer and my muscles grow bigger faster."

Paul goes on to point out that the arms do not need to stop growing. "Someone asked me once if I thought I could make my arms any bigger. I told him to just watch what happens. In 1993, I put a half-inch on my arms for the Arnold Classic. I was able to do that because of my instinctive training. Just remember that the body can become a creature of habit. As long as you stay creative and constantly do things in your workout to shock your body it will never get stale or stop improving."

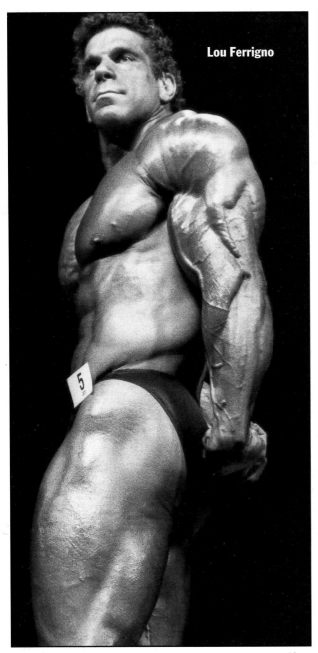

Lou Ferrigno

Biceps
Seated alternate dumbell curls
• Curl the dumbell up with your right hand, keeping your palm in until the dumbell has passed your thigh, then turn your palm up for the remainder of the curl.
• As you lower the dumbell, keep your palm up until the dumbell has passed your thigh, then turn your palm in.
• Repeat the movement with your left arm.
• Keep your upper arm close to your side at all times. Perform both exercises for 5 sets of 8 repetitions.

Heavy-duty Biceps Blowout [11]
One Set!
Dorian Yates got together with Mike Mentzer for some biceps-training advice. What Mike had Dorian do was very interesting. Mike related the scene in an issue of *Ironman*:

Mohamed Makkawy

Bill Pearl's Fantastic Arm Routine [10]
Bill Pearl, five-time Mr. Universe, was one of the top champions of all-time. In fact, he still looks fantastic. At 5'10", he had a pair of 21-inch arms. His arm-training advice for intermediate-level bodybuilders is:
Triceps:
Standing EZ-curl barbell French curls
• Use the narrowest hand spacing possible on the EZ-curl.
• Keep your upper arms stationary and close to your head.
• You can also do this exercise seated and using a medium grip.

"When Dorian Yates was in Los Angles five months prior to the 1992 Mr. Olympia, he told me that he was not satisfied with his progress. He had allowed the number of sets he was performing for each bodypart to creep up to six. Although he was reluctant to accept my conclusion that he was overtraining, he did allow me to supervise his biceps workout that day. The biceps workout consisted of one set on the Nautilus curl machine carried to failure, at which point I helped him into the fully contracted position and had him hold it there for 15 seconds, before lowering under strict control.

Mike Mentzer

Dorian didn't say much other than he liked the tremendous pump – and with that, he left the gym. Thinking the matter was closed, I was surprised to see Dorian the next morning at Gold's Gym, eagerly seeking me out. 'Mike' he said, 'I wouldn't be here talking to you now, but I swear, I woke up this morning and my biceps were bigger.' "

As you can see, there are a great variety of styles when it comes to the way the super stars train their arms. Some use massive amounts of sets, and others use as few as one set. The repetitions vary also. This chapter provided you with a smorgasbord of muscular training for the arms. Use *Super Routines of the Super Stars* to choose some new routines to try out.

1) Flex Wheeler, "Bigger and Better" *Flex (*May 1996), 61.

2) Mike Francois, "Ungodly Guns" *Flex (*January 1996), 52.

3) Steve Davis, "Mo' Muscle" *Ironman (*April 1996), 76.

4) Skip LaCour, "Natural Mass Machine" *Ironman (*April 1996), 66

5) Shawn Ray, "Biceps, Pro Style" *Flex* (March 1996), 197.

6) Carol Ann Weber, "The Real Deal with Evander Holyfield" *Muscular Development (*December 1995), 101.

7) Paul Dillett, "Feeling It" *Flex* (November 1995), 172.

8) Lou Ferrigno, "Head to Head" *Flex* (November 1995), 222.

9) Chris Lund, "Watching Makkawy Train Arms and Shoulders" *MuscleMag International* (January 1982), 36.

10) Bill Pearl with David Prokop, "20 Months to a Champion Physique" *Ironman* (October 1994), 46.

11) Mike Mentzer, "Heavy Duty Excerpt," *Ironman* (September 1994), 99.

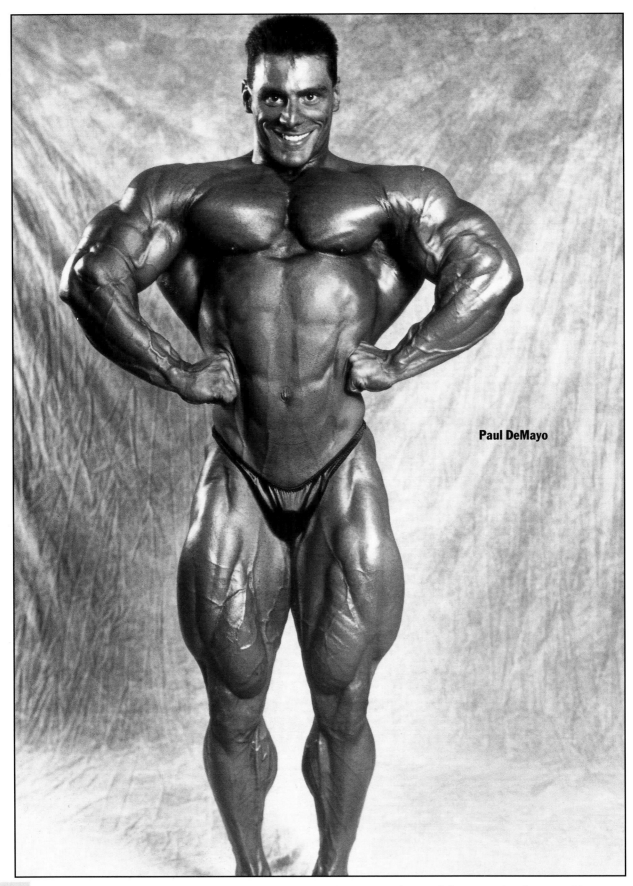

Paul DeMayo

CHAPTER FIVE

Leg-training Cycles

completely developed with full symmetry – no imbalance. The champion bodybuilders give each aspect of their legs a full workout. Their quads, hamstrings, and calves are all blasted into submission. The super stars use specific training cycles for shaping their legs.

This chapter will focus on the lower body – how the stars train their legs from all angles. Check out the super routines of the super stars with a focus on the legs.

Quadzilla's Calf Advice [1]

• Going heavy isn't as important as focusing directly on the calf and only on the calf. Start with a lighter weight until you get the true feel and correct form, then increase the poundage.

• Higher reps are best – 15 to 25. Go for the burn.

• Always stretch between sets.

• Train calves with as much intensity as you give your larger muscle groups, and be consistent.

Leg-training is tough. Some people like it and a lot of others don't – they view it as a necessary evil. Whatever your view, you can get some real insight from an overview of the leg-training of the champions. To compete at the level where they have risen to, you have to know your business when it comes to the legs. The legs have to be

Hard work pays off for Kevin Levrone.

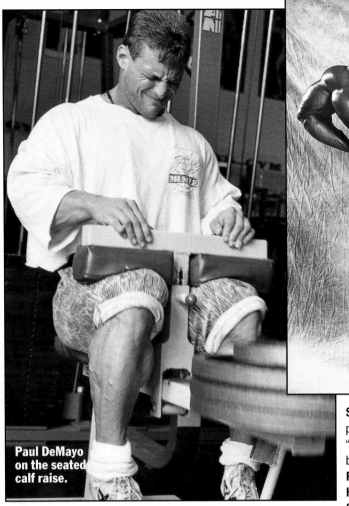

Paul DeMayo on the seated calf raise.

Quadzilla's legs would not be spectacular if he hadn't focused on symmetry as well as size.

Hack squats: 5 to 10 sets of 15 to 20 repetitions
Lunges: 3 to 5 sets of 10 repetitions for each leg
Lying leg curls: 5 sets of 8 to 10 repetitions, plus lighter pyramid set of 10 sets
Seated leg curls: 5 sets of 8 to 10 repetitions
Stiff-leg deadlifts: 5 sets of 8 to 10 repetitions
Rod spends about two hours of training on his upper legs.

Charles Glass' Leg-blast Cycle [4]

Leg extensions: 4 sets of 15 to 20 repetitions, light to moderate weight
Seated leg presses: 4 sets of 15 reps, heavy weights, performed at various angles, full range
"Robby (Robinson) and I don't let each other cheat because we both know how bad we want it."
Reverse hack squats: 4 sets of 15 reps, heavy weights
Hack squats: 4 sets of 15 reps superset with lunges
Squats: 4 sets of 5 to 7 reps, heavy weights
Calves trained on a separate day with:
Standing calf raises: 3 or 4 sets of 15 to 20 repetitions
Donkey calf raises: 3 or 4 sets of 15 to 20 repetitions
Seated calf raises: 3 or 4 sets of 15 to 20 repetitions

Mike O'Hearn's Leg Cycle [2]

Squats: 1x5x135, 1x5x225, 1x5x315, 1x5x405, 1x5x505, 1x5x600, 1x5x650 (powerlifting suit and knee wraps added), 1x3x700, 1x3x750, 1x2x800.
Leg Presses: 1x8x1000, 1x8x1500, 1x8x2000, 1x8x2500, then 200 pounds stripped each time he hit failure until no more weight is on the machine.
Leg Extensions: 3 sets of 30 repetitions
This routine is performed once a week.
Calves are trained daily for 5 sets of 20 repetitions. Hamstrings are trained on a separate day.
To support his heavy lifting, Mike eats 10,000 to 12,000 calories per day.

Rod Ketchen's Killer Quads & Hamstrings [3]

Leg extensions: 5 warmup sets of 10 to 15 repetitions, 10 sets of 8 to 10 repetitions. Performed in slow motion, holding the contraction for a two-count.

Start

Shawn Ray's Off-season Upper-leg Cycle [5]

Leg presses: 4 sets of 12 to 15 repetitions
Rear squats: 4 sets of 12 to 15 repetitions
Leg extensions: 4 sets of 12 to 15 repetitions
Leg curls: warmup: 3 sets of 12 to 15 repetitions, 5 sets of 12 to 15 repetitions
Stiff-leg deadlifts occasionally used in place of the leg curls

Shawn advises that "throughout your career you should constantly change the order of your exercises, play with the repetitions, and play with the poundages. If you consistently stick with the same poundages and the same order of exercises, you'll constantly look the same."

Lee Labrada's Killer Calf Cycle [6]

Toe presses on leg-press machine: "Always get a full contraction and as long a stretch as possible."
Seated calf raises: "You want to get as large a range of motion as possible. Constant tension, constant movement, no rest! The important thing is to stretch all the way down and all the way up. Most people don't go down far enough. Make sure you use as full a range of motion as possible on each rep."
Standing calf raises: "I use a medium pace and sometimes slow motion. You have to be very careful if you're using heavy weights in this exercise. Never come down too fast or use jerky movements – you can rip your Achilles' tendon."

Variety is the spice of life, and the key to great muscle gains.
– Shawn Ray

Shawn Ray works his legs with leg presses.
Start

Finish

Lee stretches after each and every set. He also points out that "most of your calf size comes from the soleus, which responds best to reps of 15 or higher."

Dave Fisher's Leg Cycle [7]

Dave Fisher's leg-training is basic and hard. His thigh-training workout includes:
Squats: up to 9 sets pyramiding down to a single or triple
Hack squats: 5 sets of 12 to 20 repetitions
45-degree leg presses: 5 sets of 12 to 20 repetitions
For hamstrings, Dave does leg curls and stiff-leg deadlifts. He performs 6 sets of the lying leg curls and 3 or 4 sets of the stiff-leg deadlifts.

Dave does 45 minutes of calf work. (He does not train them on the same day as quad and hamstring workouts.) He performs standing calf

Everything including diet must be factored into your cycle.
– Mike O'Hearn

Leg presses
Finish

raises, seated calf raises, and toe presses on the leg-press machine. He normally performs 12 to 15 sets for the calves, but sometimes goes as high as 50 repetitions.

Bruce Lee's Leg Workout[8]

Squats: Bruce practiced many variations of the squat. He often would perform 2 sets of 12 repetitions of the squat, taking only a short breather between sets. He performed squats in the full-squat method.

Evander Holyfield's Leg Workout[9]

Leg extensions: 4 sets of 12 repetitions
Front squats: 4 sets of 8 repetitions
Leg curls: 3 sets of 10 repetitions
Stiff-leg deadlifts: 2 sets of 8 to 10 repetitions
All exercises are performed in an explosive manner. He also does road work and jumping rope.

Squats
Start

Rod Ketchens

J.J. Marsh's Monster Thigh Routine[10]

Leg extensions: 2 sets of 15 to 20 repetitions at each weight amount, (60, 100, 150, 200 and 250 pounds). J.J. says, "I always do these first. I want plenty of blood in my legs and around my knees before going to the heavier exercises."
Smith-machine squats: 2 sets of 15 to 20 repetitions at each weight amount, (135, 225, 315, 405, and 495 pounds).
Front squat on Smith machine: 2 sets of 15 to 20 repetitions at each of 135, 225, 315, and 405 pounds.
Hack squats: 15 reps with four plates (45 pounds) per side, 15 reps with five plates per side, and 10 repetitions with 6 plates per side.
Leg presses: 15 repetitions with 750 pounds, working up to 10 repetitions with 1100 pounds.
Dumbell lunges: A variety of lunges from different angles.
Hamstrings are trained with straight-leg deadlifts.

Finish

Dave Fisher sticks to the basics and ups the intensity to develop his professional-quality legs.

Pete Miller's Thick Thigh Routine[11]

Quads:

Leg presses: Warmups, then 5 or 6 sets of 20 to 30 repetitions superset with sissy squats or occasionally Smith machine or regular squats.

Hamstrings:

Straight-leg deadlifts: 5 sets of high repetitions (sometimes up to 40 repetitions per set!).

Pete tenses his hamstrings as he works them with the straight-leg deadlift. Pete says leg curls don't give his legs the burn he wants — "nothing feels as good as straight-leg deadlifts."

Skip LaCour's Leg Cycle[12]

Hamstrings and quads:

Standing leg curls: 2 warmup sets of 8 to 12 repetitions

Leg presses: 1 warmup set of 6 to 8 repetitions, 2 heavy sets of 4 to 6 repetitions

Dave Fisher

J.J. Marsh

Seated calf raises: 3 sets of 12 to 30 repetitions
Donkey raises: 3 sets of 12 to 30 repetitions
Another routine:
Calf-machine extensions: 3 sets of 12 to 30 repetitions
Standing calf raises: 3 sets of 12 to 30 repetitions
The weight and repetitions are pyramided up on each set for both routines.

"Every third workout, I select one exercise and do six to eight sets, pyramiding up for the first four sets, then back down for the remaining sets."

Get plenty of blood flowing through your legs before doing heavy work. – J.J. Marsh on the leg-press machine.

Start

Stiff-leg deadlifts: 2 heavy sets of 4 to 6 repetitions
Lying leg curls: 2 sets of 6 to 8 repetitions
Calves:
Seated calf raises: 1 warmup set of 12 to 15 repetitions, 3 sets of 10 to 12 repetitions
Standing calf raises: 2 sets of 12 to 15 repetitions.

Sonbaty's Super Calf Cycle[13]

"At my most shredded, dehydrated, lowest-bodyfat contest condition, my calves still measure more than 21 inches cold." So says Nasser El Sonbaty, the man who almost took the title out of Dorian Yates' hands in the 1995 Mr. Olympia. His routine is as follows:

Personal Experimentation

The training routines of the champions provide information, insight, and especially inspiration for your own training. You can gain much by studying what the stars do to build their size, strength, and shape. Check out the various routines in this book and try some of them out in your own training approach. Notice the different training philosophies of the champions and the results the stars have individually achieved from the various training cycles they use. Develop your own training cycle concepts but always be willing to try something new and different. Who knows, it may be the key you are looking for. Give more than one workout approach a fair trial. Use the brief, heavy-duty approach for a while, then try the multi-set workout. Experiment until you find what works best for you. And use *Super Routines of the Super Stars* as your guide.

Finish

Nasser El Sonbaty shows the excellent results he gained by using a super routine.

1) Ask Quadzilla, *Ironman* (September 1994), 130.

2) Lonnie Teper, "Mike O'Hearn, Bodybuilding's Kool Kat" *Ironman* (October 1994), 148.

3) Reg Bradford, "Ketchens Cruches Quads & Hams!" *Muscular Development* (March 1996), 106.

4) Carol Ann Weber, "Star Trainer Charles Glass Shines" *Muscular Development* (March 1996), 159.

5) T.C. Luoma, "Hail Ray, King of the Lunges" *MuscleMag International* (July 1991), 142.

6) Rosemary Hallum, "Killer Calves" *MuscleMag International* (July 1991), 102.

7) Dave Fisher and Greg Zulak, "Squats, Squats, and More Squats," *MuscleMag International* (February 1995), 67.

8) John Little, "Warm Marbles," *Ironman* (April 1996), 91.

9) Carol Ann Weber "The Real Deal" *Muscular Development* (December 1995), 101.

10) Gayle Hall, "J.J. Marsh...the 3:30 a.m. Warrior" *MuscleMag International* (December 1990), 54.

11) T.C. Luoma, "My 30-inch America Thighs" *MuscleMag International* (March 1991), 40.

12) Skip La Cour, "Natural Mass Machine" *Ironman* (April 1996), 70.

13) Nasser El Sonbaty, "Wean Your Calves" *Flex* (January 1996), 74.

Index

Photo Index

Contributing Photographers
Jim Amentler, John Butler, Paula Crane,
Irvin Gelb, Robert Kennedy, Jason Mathas,
Nailon, Mitsuru Okabe